Deep Blue

Colin Richard Mansell

chipmunkapublishing
the mental health publisher

Colin Richard Mansell

All rights reserved, no part of this publication may be reproduced by any means, electronic, mechanical photocopying, documentary, film or in any other format without prior written permission of the publisher.

      Published by
      Chipmunkapublishing
      PO Box 6872
      Brentwood
      Essex CM13 1ZT
      United Kingdom

http://www.chipmunkapublishing.com

Copyright © Colin Richard Mansell 2010

Chipmunkapublishing gratefully acknowledge the support of Arts Council England.

Deep Blue

About the Author

Since writing this book I have become a counselor I did my diplomas at Lambeth College I have gained a level 1 and 2 CPCAB status of qualification and am now in my 3rd year, I believe that poetry is a form of counseling, It can heal the mind and bring peace to our lives, I also work with the homeless, ex offenders, mentally ill, the elderly and with people that have learning problems, I offer advice, friendship and counseling, I help them and in doing so, this helps me.

Colin Richard Mansell

Deep Blue

JOSH MY SON

I've not seen my son for two whole years,
And then I saw my eyes in tears.
His face, it looks so strange to me,
He had grown so tall,,, how can this be?
I sat there at the back of the bus,
Him and his mates in a world of fuss.
But then he caught a glimpse of me,
He looked so scared, why would this be?
I was a loving playful dad, never angry always glad.
His mommy told some lies about me and now he is scared to come near me.
My heart is heavy deep inside,
I use to be so full of pride.
But now I would give anything for one small kiss upon my chin.

My son Josh and his toy dog wrinks

Drug Poem
BLACK

I was in the park the other day
The park as kids where we did play

There was a man when boy I knew
We use to be a Motley crew

Now the man has blackened teeth
And blackened fingers like a thief

His eyes are set deep in his head
In fact the man looks almost dead

His eyes do stare but they can't see
I brown head don't remember me

A sad poor man is standing there
With knotted greased backed dark black hair

Deep Blue

Lucky man

Walking round in circles
What the Hell's going on
A never ending story
An ever lasting song
There's rhyme but no reason
And there's fiction but no fact
I carry too much pressure
It's going to break my back
It's picking up leaves
On a very windy day
It's a sour tasting pickle
And a boring old wet play
I must be walking on the cracks
My friend,,,
 To have all this bad, bad luck
But I'm a lucky fellow
Because I don't give a fuck

Am I Dreaming?

Just before you close your eyes
And dream a dream of lullabies
Blow a kiss to me my love
I'll feel your heart with beating blood
Sleep tight for me when I'm not
Dream deeply darling
Without a care
I care for you more than you know
Now that we've met I can't let go
If you feel the same for me
Just let me know and you will see
That my heart is dreaming too
Oh god
Am I dreaming?

Deep Blue

Bed roll

Its day one in jail
It's turned 6 o'clock
I've been interviewed
And I'm free of the dock
Bed roll and kit
Was given to me
And now it is time
For my first prison tea
Oh dearest god,,,
A cell made for three
I can't get a single,,,
For doing my time

Belmarsh has no chimneys

Santa clause please bring to me a diamond hacksaw
If you please

A set of keys would do the trick
Because I can't feel and I'm not sick
Because you see,,,
Belmarsh has no Christmas cheer
Oh Santa clause please bring to me

An overdose with a tea
This prison Santa that I'm in

Has no chimney pot to shin
So you will never get in here

To spread your loving Christmas cheers

Deep Blue

Bread

Bread, bread what kind of bread.
Long loaves, short loaves, fat ones or thins,
Round bread or flat breads, and some called tins.

Sliced bread or uncut, thin sliced or thick,
Turkish or Jewish, or a long French stick.
White bread or brown bread whole-wheat or rye,
There's enough bread here to last till I die.

Christmas

Buses are crowded with school children singing,
The shops are all busy with cash tills a ringing.
Mothers are busy, in kitchens and parlours,
The pubs are all packed with most of the fathers.
The churches are empty though bells are a tolling
This is now Christmas when no one is praying.

Deep Blue

Coldness

Have you ever ached with cold, really ached?
Old people do, do you?
They need to be kept warm, really warm,
Old people do, do you?
Chilled to the bone, the same goes,
Chilled to the bone.
Ehen the shivering, that makes the muscle ache,
When the hands and feet feel numb,
Then feel nothing at all
When hunger is no more
When time means nothing at all
When the mind drifts back and forth from fantasy
And then back to reality
When one's very soul drops, so very low
Nothing matters
My God nothing matters
The only thing that matters
Is coldness
So don't be homeless

Come dine with me

Come dine with me its bread and spuds
We only have the finest grub
We've no wine but water here
But still our cell is filled with cheer
So dine with me, my new cell mates
We eat our spoil on plastic plates
Will give our presents out at dawn
Don't be too sad
My gift is small

Deep Blue

Conscience

Walking with you, through life's troubles,
Troubling you with inner thoughts,
Keeping weariness abated
While you rest from battles fought,
Till you find that inner sanctum,
Knowing exactly where truth lies,
Helping others on their journeys
Seeing life with clear,,, true eyes,,,

Sometimes waxing, sometimes waning
Never dormant for too long,
Gently raising from the ashes,
Like some half forgotten song,
Once decided, Fixed and fearless.
Like iron train, upon the rails,
Never veering, steely steering,
Along the tracks of all life's tails.

Digging the rouble

Burning house
Open mouths
Blood red eyes
Earth that lies
Death is here
Dome is near
Death is fear
So smell the fear

Dig by hand
Frantic man
Look for child
Concrete trail
The dust it chocks
Fingers ach
Keep digging till
My back will brake
Shock sets in,,,
Dig just dig
Gods a pig
Can't dig no more,,,

Deep Blue

Funny face

Oh funny face
You make my light
You feel my wings
With wonderers flight
You bring me joy
You hold my heart
I never want to be apart
Oh funny face
With you I'm one
There is no pain to over come
God thanks you child
You hold my hand
You lead the way though
Desert sands
Oh funny face

Gas Meter

Arthur and Peter stole the gas meter,
They smuggled it out in a crate,
They returned when they'd finished,
And bought everyone's Guinness,
The customers thought they were great

Deep Blue

Happiness

Tears come from crying and from laughter too,
Money comes from working hard, and from thieving too.
Loneliness comes, when there's one,
Company when there's two.
Riches come to many folks, but happiness just a few.

Making a Brain

Take one conscience and one sub conscience brain halves and stick together remembering not to mix up left from right and up from down. Take one 12 volt battery and connect to brain plug which is located in the 11 dimensional plug Socket.
Take two eyes and with USB cable, connect to brain, if doesn't matter about left and right eyes both fit all, but make sure not to put eyes in upside down or else the world will appear up-side-down. Repeat with other four senses. Please remember I can feel a fart coming on isn't a sense. Never is, I think she fancy's me and a premature ejaculation Definitely isn't one.
 Right this is the good bit. Press the reboot button and hold for 10 seconds. You now should see a blue box saying, congratulations for buying the mark six Homo sapiens brain, release button and you're all set for life

Deep Blue

Maintenance

If you go mad or crazy during the course of three score years and ten just press the reboot button for 5 seconds warning do not remove maintenance sticker from frontal globe else you will void your brain guaranty if reboot does not work then you need to take it to mental asylum counter which is located at back of PC world once again thank you for choosing the mark 6 homo sapiens brain.

Correction maintenance to mark 6 brain dated 856AD

Some problems have appeared to some earlier models this manifests its self has blurred vision this can be corrected by the use of sand melted into discs and held on by the use of the ears this should not be attempted by anyone less than 4ft 6in tall
Thank you
Any problems call god on 0208 666 999 666 9am till 8pm closed Sundays
I THINK HESHE GO'S FISHING........

Deep Blue

Mental cloud

I feel my way
When it is dark
Hand over hand
Though life's big park
I wait the day
When I can see
When mental cloud
Will leave me be
When smoke does clear
So I can see
This mental cloud
Is killing me

Mental Mother Nature

What happens if a flower doesn't get rain?
I wonder if that flower feels any pain,
Does it feel the strain?
Or have you ever seen a sad mad rose,
When the wind blows too hard
And the rose too's and throws
Does it try and snap it's self off
Flowers don't self harm their full of charm
And love injected from the bearded man from up above
With a needle full of love
Not pain or shame
I hope that flowers are very dumb
It's sad because they will not feel the life giving sun
Oh no
I hope we're not one
We are both made from exploding suns
We can't be because I'm only scum
Not sun just scum

Deep Blue

Modern Days

Rushing ,rushing, always rushing,
Speeding cars and flashing lights.
People rushing to catch buses,
Can't touch us, we know our rights.

Sirens wailing almost daily,
Street crime up by ten per cent,
Homeless people, tired of dossing,
Worried mothers money spent.

Large stores open very early,
Never close till late at night,
Small shops going out of business,
Owners loosing in the fight.

Factory workers are on shift work,
The Only way to earn their pay.
Little workshops making craft goods,
See them failing everyday.

Colin Richard Mansell

MRS. All Alone

Listen to the lonely woman,
Walking down the cold cold street.
You can hear her talking to you,
With her aching soar poor feet.

Clippy, Cloppy, clippy, cloppy,
They begin to speak.
Mustn't stop now, mustn't stop now,
They appear to squeak to me.

Must keep moving, must keep moving,
Though I know I'm weak of this.
Soon be home now, soon be home now,
Then its time for feet to sleep.

Deep Blue

My House

It is not a country cottage, with a view across the downs,
It is not a stately mansion, just a car drive from the town.
It is not even a caravan, at the bottom of the farm,
Nor a lofty flat-let, in some converted barn.

It is my house that I live in; It is my house that I care,
Through it's just a tiny terraced thing, to part I could not bear.
I've lived there for a hundred years, or so it seems to me,
I'd rather move to China than to move away from thee.

The curtains need replacing, the carpets wearing thin,
The tiny roof is sagging, and the floor is caving in.
But the house is always cheerful, although it's very old,
And the windows, through the rattle still keep out all the cold.

It is my house that I live in; It is my house that I care,
Though it's built right in the city, and hasn't got a square.
It's just behind the bakery, just past the hippodrome,
But I love it really love it, for to me it is my home.

Not my cup of tea

The lady with hair
And funny squinty stare
She's not my cup of tea
The lady with the daughter
The one that's drinking water
Hell no she's not my cup of tea
The old bag with the voice
Drinking lap sang not through choice
She's not my cup of tea
Hold on, the lady coming in
With shopping bag fingers
And a lovely grin
Now she's the brew for me

Deep Blue

One wish

If I could have one wish, my love
I'd wish my people free of blood
No more pain and flowing tears
No more wasted blood soaked years
I saw a baby die today
Just minutes before I watched her play
But now her life has gone away
And her mother lays there weeping
Her daddy got himself a gun
For him the war had now begun
He's going to kill a soldier's son
To stop his heart from bleeding
But anyone with half a brain
Would know that war is just insane
It cannot kill this mindless pain
BECAUSE,,,, you know that we're still bleeding
So find yourself one seed of love
Washed with heavens tears of love
And maybe you'll start believing.

Panic

Crying again
Feeling the shame
Dealing with pain
Taking the strain
Walking in vain
Feeling the rain
I'm still in pain
Want to go home
Just want to go home
God take me home
Please don't make me roam.

Deep Blue

Drug poem
Pin head

The gear
The fear
The junky little queer
Arms like a pin cushion
Bladder full of beer
Eyes like pins
Heart full of sins
You never go to sleep at night
Unless you prick your skin
Drug River is your vanes
The gear just fuels your pains
Your life it is a joke
I bet you'll cut your throat
Eyes full of blood red tears
I'll help you face your fears
Pin head

Prison poems

Some of my book was written about prison, I work a lot with ex offenders, so I would like to draw your attention to the plight of quite a high percentage of prisoners in and out of UK jails with some form of mental illness, there's no such thing has a happy prisoner,,,, conditions can range from mild depression to suicide, and sadly often does. You see,,, everybody thinks their sentence is a "long one" for example, a young man gets "banged up", it's his first time in jail, but unlucky for him he had committed a crime in Woolwich in South East London and this means the first time offender gets sent to the infamous Belmarsh which the locals like to call "Hellmarsh", a category A prison.

A first time offender will be spending his first night in the company of murderers ,terrorists and a whole nest of drug addicted petty offenders which are " coming down" from a whole cocktail of different drugs. The heroin addicts will be sheeting and pissing themselves as they go "cold turkey", the alcoholics will be sweating, sleeping and craving sugar and this is all happening in a room approximately two metres by three meters and you'll be lucky if you can open the window more than ten centimetres and, believe me, this is not enough for three sweaty prisoners .This will be the status quo for the next two or three days.

Our young friend will be suffering and his friends and family on the outside might not even know that he is in jail, he will be felling frightened, remorseful and confused. Although you get one phone call on arrival this often ends without making contact with any of your love ones because you have had your mobile phone taken from you and put into storage and who of us can remember phone numbers these days? Generally it

Deep Blue

takes about a week to sort out your phone numbers and get your first weeks" canteen" which will include tobacco and a few other basic provisions. I believe that this can be the most vulnerable time for a new prisoner and some people just can't face it, so they start to contemplate however many weeks, months or years they have to spend in this God forsaken hell whole, which is prison.

Reincarnation

Reincarnation, secondary plane,
Mirror image, look alikees,
Seemingly the same,
Past becoming present,
Yesterday is today,
Tomorrow has already been,
In a different kind of way.

Daylight follows night,
With night becoming day,
As birth follows death,
In another sort of way,
Life is rekindled in many different forms,
Each has its beginning,
Each has its own dawn.

Deep Blue

Remembrance

The fireplace is empty the cupboard bare,
There's not a soul in the town that really does care.
Though she's lived there a lifetime she died in despair,
For there's not a kind soul who really does care.

She use to be famous and important to many,
She never had a thought for saving a penny.
She paraded her wealth and flaunted her money,
To all that would listen and to her there were many.

She gave great parties and arranged many balls,
She organised church fetes and helped on the stalls,
She gave many lectures to societies and clubs,
She donated freely to the scouts, guides and cubs.

But then she became bankrupt and was brought before court,
She pleaded quite strongly it wasn't her fault,
She relied on compassion but this was denied,
It was after this ruling that sadly she died.

Her grave is abandoned no cross and no stone,
No memorial garden she lies there alone.
Though her life was so happy she had all that she wished,
She lies there forgotten and never be missed.

Colin Richard Mansell

Silence

It's quiet, very quiet.
Is that a car I hear?
Is it stopping?
No, it's going,
There's another...
No, it's gone,
It's quiet, so very quiet.

Shall I turn the wireless on?
No, I don't feel like music.
Listen, I can hear the children going past
What a noise, all that shouting,
All that whistling, all that laughing,
They're happy, so very happy.

I remember when I was young,
But that's a long time ago now,
Oh, I'm so glad, and so tired,
And it's quiet again now,
It's quiet, so very, very quiet.

Deep Blue

Sitting

I'm sitting waiting for my train
The people's faces look the same
I have to do this for twenty years
The thought of this brings me to tears
I work each day just like a dog
A never ending horrid slog
Two weeks holiday once a year
On Friday night we have a beer
Is this what life is all about
I role around and scream and shout
I want more, just a little more
My life is such a bore,
I really need more.

Sky

Sky of love
Sky so bright
Dad will snug you in the night
Sky so deep
Sky so blue
I'll spread my love all over you
My darling, darling little girl
I miss your touch
I miss your smell
So tell your mum to hold you tight
And snug you deeply in the night

.

Deep Blue

Spring

On boundless grass, the primrose dance,
The robin is heard to sing,
The winter is gone, the days are long,
Oh, Glorious joy of spring.

In wooded combs, the bluebell blooms,
The lambs on high meadows play,
The cold has gone, the sun grows strong,
The summer is coming our way.

On bubbling streams, the moonlight gleams,
The frogs are starting to spawn,
The air is fresh, the owl will nest,
 The Earth is being reborn.

The Lonely Christmas Fire

Sitting in the armchair by the open fire,
Waiting for the postman's knock, or not, as it transpired.
Thinking of my family gone, to different sites and towns,
Wonder who would visit me, or invite to "come around".

Sitting in the armchair by the open fire,
Thinking of a lovely meal, with Christmas pudd, on fire!
Opening all the presents whilst listening to the sounds.
The children sing, the church bells ring, the cold wind upon the downs.

Sitting in the armchair by the open fire,
Knowing that I haven't much, but at least I'm not a liar.
Wondering if someone would call, my grandson is like a clown.
Small ones take my hand, and lead me down to a night out on the town.

Sitting in the armchair by the open fire,
Remembering all the games we played, of which we never tire
And all those happy hours we spent, whilst sitting all around,
Playing "Blind man's bluff", "Turkey's duff" and "Donkey on the ground"

But now it's dark and lonely and there isn't any fire,
There is no one who came to call, to lift my spirit higher.
I'm all alone, but what cares have I, as is very often found.
It's pleasant just to sit and dream
Because dreams can't make a sound.

Deep Blue

Trapped Mother Nature

Trapped in this body, with a sick mind that wants to be free
That hollow feeling of hell not love is washing over me
The darkness is here now, and so is the fear now
So break out the beer now and the drugs make it free
I'm having a wake for my soul that does ache
I do this most nights Since my wife set me free
I wonder who comes Mr. Hope has just rang
And that's him of the list I knew it would be.
There's Mr. Fear and despair They're combing their hair
The flash little ghosts They are frightening me
There's suicide Pete
With his suit smart and neat
He wants to come over and start talking to me
I'm frightened he will He might give me a pill
Then the party will end
Just you wait and see
A hangover I need
A sprinkling of weed
And gods big bright soul
So please hear my plea
It's a funny old life
Now I've lost my kids and my wife
Oh please god
Explain why you're shitting on me.

Understanding Mental Illness

Being mentally ill can be very scary and lonely so show a little kindness and empathy. If you are suffering for mental illness on any level be it depression or a more severe form of mental illness I urge you to seek out some help which can take many forms, you might self disclose your situation to a close friend or relative, you could talk to your GP and he may be able to refer you to your local counselling service, there you will find a non-judgemental and empathetic people from all walks of life. They generally are the more mature range of people and they have lead a very full life and it always helps to talk.

There is no shame in mental illness, it's not something we want or ask for and no one is guilty for this so, admit it and get some professional help, don't forget ,life is a gift and truth is love. May you find peace and happiness and all what you need to cleanse your soul.

Deep Blue

Underworld

Black eyes
Cruel skies
Twisted lies
Sad good byes
Dogs that bark
Broken hearts
All these things
That shapes my heart
The fearful child
The sadist smile
The crying girl
The underworld

Window Warrior of Belmarsh

On first night in jail
You must listen well
To window warriors
They're misunderstood

"Oh, John boy, you got a burn"?

Billy, old son
Are you on my spur?

They shout and they hollow
All night long
Playfully singing their
Warrior songs
They shout out the windows
To old friends and new
Knowing this action will piss off the" screws,,
They vent their frustration into the air
With their warrior songs and their pain redden stare.

Deep Blue

Contradictions of the heart

How can you make my heart beat twice as fast and stop it at the same time
I say my heart isn't made of glass, so it won't shatter
It doesn't mean you should get a hammer and see if that will break it
I said be honest and open with me and all will be fine
Because I know myself, and I know that I can deal with what I feel
You say you don't want to hurt me but you can't hurt anyone as much as you did to me
They say don't give pain and tears to those with a good heart
I've shed enough tears to fill an ocean with the pain you have caused
You say you care for me and I am perfect
How can I be when you don't even respect me?
You distance yourself from me thinking I'm oblivious to it
I noticed everything; I was giving you a chance to stop hurting me
You want to have your cake and eat it at too
But if you eat the cake then you want more or a different flavour
If I believed in the stars I wouldn't utter a word
Life is too long when I'm not with you
But life falls short when I'm with you
Why are you so adamant to see if I bleed, if I'm like everyone else?
They say the only time someone doesn't care is when the love is gone
You say you're sweet and you don't hurt anyone
How can you, when you don't even act honestly towards me?
I don't think you can ever make up for the pain you have caused me
Why did you do that or maybe that's who you always

were, a ruthless carnivore?
I see the best in you, so why do you always bring hurt to the party?
Am I the fool that pays the price of trust and faith?
Maybe the day will come when I can no longer afford your love
When you break the heart of someone too many times
The pieces become rounded as they fall to the floor
And one day they will no longer fit back together again
I cannot forgive you for the wrong that you have done
But what can I do if I still love you?
Why?

Why is it every time you kiss me, you make me dizzy..........from the very first time
Why do I forget about the whole world when I'm with you?
It's been one year since you kissed me and not a single day has passed without you in my mind,
Every morning I wake up and I think of you, why?
Every night before I go to sleep, I think of you...why?
I don't even remember my dreams because all I think about, is you
No matter how much I keep busy you keep pestering me whatever I do....
You keep popping up in my head!
I can't do anything!
What kind of madness is that?
All I want is you, nothing else but you
You make me smile from the inside out
All I have to do is hear your voice, get your text or see you and I'm happy beyond words
I wish I could die before we have to part, because I don't want to know how it feels
When I'm not with you
I feel so much pain with the thought of not being with you, how am I supposed to live without you?

Deep Blue

You complete me and I can't even say I love you anymore
 Because what I feel for you is beyond that
What am I suppose to do? Help me!
Tell me how you do it, I want to be like you, switch off like you!

The face that I adore

The face that would hold my gaze,
The one I couldn't take my eyes off,
The one that my eyes would never tire of
The one I could not get enough of

What happened?

My gaze doesn't want to glance there
My eyes won't look up at your face
I can't bear to see the face that I adored

What happened?

I don't like what I see it stings at me
The pain won't go away the wound just won't heal

What happened?

I'm trying to heal my pains, but you keep tearing at it
I'm moving away from you and you don't even realise
You're a fool to yourself

Deep Blue

Killing me with your silence

I feel like I have committed a crime,
Is it so bad to love you?
Is it so bad to want you?
Is it so bad to need you?
Is it so bad to think of you?
Is it so bad to be happy?

A crime was committed
Of falling in love with you,
Of wanting you from the bottom of my heart,
Of needing and yearning for you,
Of thinking about you day and night
Or being happy with you.

Now I must be punished for my crime
For falling in love with you,
For wanting you,
For needing you,
For having no thoughts but you,
For being happy with you.

How will I pay for my crime?
Because I'm not sorry, I love you!

Because I still want you,
Because I still need you,
Because I still think about you,
Because I still feel happy for being with you

Colin Richard Mansell

How will you punish me for my crime?

By saying you don't love me?
By saying you don't want me?
By saying you don't need me?
By saying you don't think about me?
By saying you was not happy with me?

Or will you just simply kill me slowly with your silence?

Deep Blue

Hokey cokeee

You put the sharp end in; you take the sharp end out,
In out in out you jab it all about.
Then you sniff some hokey cokeee and you fall right down.

Is that what life's all about
oooooooh the hokey cokeee cokeee
oooooooh the hokey cokeee cokeee
oooooooh the hokey cokeee cokeee

You put some brown shit in; you take some red blood out,
In out in out you splash it all about.
The kitchen's full of blood now and there's no doubt.

Is that what life's about
oooooooh the hokey cokeee cokeee
Wake up in the night all soaky soaky soaky
My bones feel like they brokey brokey brokey
Lips clenched, Arms bent ra ra ra

Shopping with Gordon

I wish Gordon brown was a good friend of mine
We'd go out for lunch and drink the finest red wine
A shopping trip next I think it would be
Id bring all my friends we'd spend money for free
To be a MPs would be too good to be true
What a fantastic job
To screw me then screw you
I think Mr Wordsworth would spin in his grave
I wonder how much the spin doctors will save
So god bless old England
How much does that cost
I don't think it matters
Now that MP's are toffs

Deep Blue

Sick soul

I waited for my sun to shine
I waited for a taste
I want this body to be fine
Because I am sick and tired
Of feeling sick and tired
This illness of the soul
Takes my mind
It takes control
I'm frightened of myself, you see?
I am scared of what I've tried to be
Because all I ever wanted,
I wanted to be free.
I want you to want me

Distant love

E.S.P.
Please my darling send to me
The ghost that lies within your soul
Your faith I seek, I love you so
Send it through the sky at night
Through heavens breathe
Just like a kite
I'll leave my window just ajar
So it will blow into my heart
And take my breath away

Deep Blue

South Bank lunch

I'm standing at the South Bank
On a love filled sunny day
The Thames is full to brimming
All the people are out to play
Train rattles over bridge on left
Wind blowing though my hair
With this very London poem
Of which I really care
I want to write a good one
To make old London proud
With my pen I just keep pushing
Boo hoo... there floats a fluffy cloud
Here comes some dappled light
To finish off my rhyme
Of this very London poem
Of which I took my time.

Still morning

Still morning
The air is quiet
The sound of far away cars
Breaks the peace of the day
How I miss the rattle of bottles
And the way the milkman
Ruled the morning dew
I walk to the station
An every day thing
But each morning is different
A different bird sings
In a different way
In different time
One day my darling
I hope you'll be mine

Deep Blue

Stranger

I look into the eyes of a stranger
Is it you my love?
I wonder
At night, I read the evening paper
Are you there my love?
I wonder do I need to travel
To find you my love
Are you here already?
Can't I see you my love?
Are you the one I've been looking for?
If I say nothing
Will you walk out my life,
Will I ever find you again?

The gentleman

The gentleman had lost his way
When looking for some flowers,
In valley low and leafy groves
He searched with all his power
His strength runs low so he did sit
Himself beneath a tree
The dappled light was twinkling
Like stars in splendid heaven
The gentleman found peace that day
And took with him that strength away
If ever you need strength, you see,
Sit beneath a shaded tree.

Deep Blue

The locksmith

Lay your head beside mine
Dream a dream
Each door you open
May have sunshine
Or may have rain
But don't fear
Because
You will never live
Until you have tried
All keys.
So open the door
It's yours to choose
Do not be vexed by this
Because only you have the key
To your heart
You and you alone
Are the locksmith.

Colin Richard Mansell

The man in you

A story of a cup of love
Filled by heaven's dew dipped doves
She gently held my workman's hand
And said there, there I understand
If you don't want to sip my wine,
If you don't want to feel divine,
Blow of breath upon sweaty brow
And cool my soul,
And take control
But never, never be so droll
As to forget the man in you.

Deep Blue

The train and the I-pod

Train now calling
Said the bodiless voice
I got off the train
But not through choice.
Go across to the next platform
Hurry up you've been warned
So we all walk along
Like cattle been scorned
Hurry up hurry
I'm goanna be late
So I push through the cows
To the front of the gate
And I find a small seat
And I fan myself
Through the sweatiest heat
Finally we're moving
So I plug in my wire
The grove is so good
That I start to catch fire
My book goes up inflames
In front of my face
I start nodding my head
Like I'm out of my face.

The way

I love it when you touch my hand
I love you because you understand
You play the game of love so well
I love the way your perfume smells
You are to me a guiding light
I'll squeeze and snug your body tight
Your smiling face it drives me wild
My loving playful dreaming child
I'll spend my time, my life with you
You'll never fill a day of blue
Because of you I'm full of pride
One day, my love, you'll be my bride
So come with me to star filled night
My dreamy red cheeked wilful bride.

Deep Blue

Sons

To my sons,
To my future
Let go my sons of all your pain now
Take a breath and let go
The fault was not yours
So don't take no blame, my beautiful sons
Your dad is with you
I am you,
I run within your veins,
I am every other beat of your heart
I come to you when you are asleep
Dad forever more,
For this, my sons, I'm sure!

Two friends lay

One man and his dog
Nestled like two twins in the womb
Surrounded by crumbs
With crumbs on there beards
And crumbs in there hair
The dog didn't care
Oh, the dog did not care
The man was sleeping but,
He still had enough consciousness
To finger the ears of old Rex.
All most like rolling a fag, quite rough
Rex puffed with ecstasy
His back leg peddled like a man on a bike
As they lay in the night
Waiting for the first rays of morn
Dreaming the same dream
Because they were a team
Forever till death do they part?
But never apart
Because they are one,
One man and his dog.

Deep Blue

Waking in jail

When I wake up in the night
I dream myself right by your side
I say a little prayer for you
And hope that you will hear me too,
The nights are long, the days are hard
I feel your love inside my heart
And hope the fire burns so bright
To keep you safe and warm at night
Never let the flames burn dim
It will keep me strong till I get out,
So, keep dreaming of me as I will of you,
Can't wait for the day when one becomes two.

Colin Richard Mansell

You smell the roses sweeter than me

Joy and pain it's all the same
Just like a flower needs the rain.
If you see your mother die
Then surely that will make you cry
But when you see your baby born
Then you will feel that extra warm
Because life, you see, is good and bad
There's nothing wrong in feeling sad.

Deep Blue

Alive

Peaceful minds,
Sunny days,
Love, health and laughter
Riches of the Earth,
Things of truth and worth,
Babies being born,
A mother's touch at dawn,
The little girl who cries
A feeling deep inside,
A friend that comes to help,
A shiver down your spine,
The dawn bird that sings,
These are all the things
That makes me feel alive.

Jail Induction

Three in a cell
Oh, my God, what a smell!
The food gives you wind
The tobacco is hell
It's that red bull old crap
It's induction, you see,
And the cupboards are bare
And there are only two chairs
I eat on my bunk
Because the food is so junk,
The tea bags are dust
Oh, God it's unjust
First week inside, you're on veggie rations
You see,
That's a baked potato to you
And an onion for me.
What a happy life for us free!

Deep Blue

Can I?

Can I have some
Gold,
Love,
Smarts,
Fast, fast cars,
Cheeky chops,
A nice little watch,
Sex on the beach,
A juicy pink peach
A rub to my feet?

Can I have some
 Loyal good chum,
A really nice bum
A grade one blonde bird
A regular turd
Shoes that fit
A girl with great tits
Some fish and some chips?
I don't want a job
And I'm not a slob
My ears are not big
I don't want some,

But I do have fat hips
And a spot on my chin
Where should I begin?

Can I have some?
Do you want some too?

Changing Man

Life changing sunrise
Last night the devil blew his breath on me
Inhale pain, exhale love
Like the sun I too need to rise
Above God's clouds
With hope and pride
Scared soul,
Scared body,
Scared mind,
Life changing sunrise
I need to change
Inhale peace, exhale hope
The moment comes
But just like that
It's gone again
Inhale love, exhale joy
Peace is born from inside heaven.

Deep Blue

Daddy

As cold as new laid snow
As peaceful as the doe
Glistening like the lake of life
I'll tuck you in your bed at night
So peaceful sleep my starlight child
I'll dream a dream of warmth and gold
I'll hold you tight when you are cold
So lay in daddy's arms, my son,
This dream is yours
Your dreams have come
Because daddy loves you,
My lovely son!

Colin Richard Mansell

Dreams

Sugar of the soul,
Power of the heart,
Blood pumping through my veins,
Diamonds in my eyes
I'm not in prison when I dream
My soul's not locked inside this cell
I can fly away to anywhere when I dream
So, keep my body here, my friend!
Please, keep me in here till the end
I want to dream you can't change that
I want to fly just like a bat!
I'll fly into the sky at night
My dreams will be my one delight!

Deep Blue

Fair Weather Friend

The fair weather friend
Likes sunny warm days
And they hate rain and thunder
They hate snow and haze
They are a strange breed of person
Because they can't stand a fuss
The fair weather friend
Will be strange on the bus
When trouble and strife
Comes a calling for you
Those fair weather friends
Are a bad friend for you

Fast life

Lost at sea
Can't see the land
The wood from the trees
Lost keys in the sand
Need glasses, you see
The glasses of life
Now I can't see
My kids and my wife
Drink water not wine
And don't drive too fast
Else you won't see passion
The passion of life

Deep Blue

Gone now

Round and round
My head it goes
This hurtful dream
Of yesterday
Watch and see the children play
Be quick they only play when I'm sleeping
My wife, she had a pie for me
It was so nice a treat to see,
Just like a dream
It turned into a kiss
And did you see my fans downstairs
Having a lovely time
I've awoke now and it's gone
Because birds only sing in heaven.

Labyrinth

In the labyrinth of life
Two kids
A job
And a loving wife
And then you find yourself in jail
Asking questions why? and how?
And now you miss your kids and wife
You need to find a path in life
So use the stars to navigate
In life, you see, it's never too late
So twinkle, twinkle little star
A whole new life is not so far.

Deep Blue

Long Night

Another sleepless night
My soul and conscience fight
I toss and turn
Because my heart burns
I long to see the light
This trouble that I'm in
Saps my life and love within
Without the love
From up above
I don't know where to begin
I can't communicate
The words don't come out straight
I can't go on
With this sad song
I think my soul will break.

Colin Richard Mansell

Play the game

If you find yourself in jail
Do not fight screws, tooth and nail
Because they could be a friend to you
Or they could really twist the screw
Never ever push the bell
Because that will really cause you hell
Just play the game
And you'll be fine
And find a way to pass your time.

Deep Blue

Quiet time (say a little prayer for me)

Who grieves God's heart anymore?

The masses who feed their loneliness and longings,
Their unsustainable hunger and thirst,
On the World's hollow scraps?

Or we, his well-fed children,
Who hide our source of sustenance?
The living water and bread of life,
As though he was a private delight?

God's all- sufficient son

Is meant to be shared,
Come to the table and meet my Jesus,
Feast on his eternal riches,
Let's tell the world.

Remember

Remember me
The man of your dreams
The man who took your heart
At the time we was one

Deep Blue

A stone is born

When spring water freezes it is hard like stone
When a heart breaks it turns to stone, hard cold stone
Powerful running water takes the sharpness from stone
Stone is made by time alone
But time alone can't make stone
You need earth and tuff and crushed sand
And God's builders hand to bring the stone to life
But stone is dead it lays upon its bed
And it wares away from the very day it was born
The earth gives birth to stone
It can be born from the fire and from the belly of God's earth
That's when the stone is fluid ,it runs
It comes like hot sticky toffee down mountains to the sea
We have always and forever been in the Stone Age
From afar a stone looks dead but instead try and look real close
Use a lens unlike most and you will see the majesty of stone
Upon the stone is life, you see it's been there for eternity
You see the wealth of life upon that stone.

Let's go mad

Sitting at my desk
Clock watching
Palm on chin
Face like a smacked arse
Terminally grumpeeeee
I think I will go mad for a bit
Or have I still got time?
See, all that clock watching
And now there's no time to go mad
I don't know I need to be more like a funny clown
Look into his eyes
See what I mean
Mad with a capital M.

Deep Blue

Moon and earth

I love you and my heart will burst
I need you like the moon needs the earth.
You are as sweet as honey dew
You know my darling I love you.
You are to me a guiding light through desert storm and jet black night.
Your eyes twinkle like diamonds.
God oh God! Your smile is so bright!
The smell of you turns me on.
It electrifies me like the sweetest song.
I am your man and you are my girl.
I would walk right through the gates of hell, through fire, brimstone and devil's mud.
The gods look down from up above, they only see your angelic face.
I loose my heart without a trace.
I hope one day you would walk with me
Through golden love clouds of ecstasy.

Dreams of childhood

Puff, puff wind
Sunny sweat days
Clouds like a puff of smoke
Filled with lemonade
Ice cream on a stick
Dip it in your tea
Leave it in there long enough
Spill it on your knees
Shepherds pie and mash
What a funny thing
Eating two potatoes
Belly like a spring
They all are dreams of childhood
That travels though my mind
They make me glad
It is so good,
So good to be alive.

Deep Blue

Hard and free

Love is hard for me
To trust and to be leave
To put my faith in you
Is what I long to do
To hold your slender hand
To find the man I am
So give love back to me
But only if it's free.

Nothings wrong

She phoned
I did not want to talk
I could hear her breath
She asked me,
"What's wrong darling?
And I said,
"If only you knew
What's rolling in my head
The tears that I've cried
The pain that I have bled
If only you knew
All the love that I have lost
If I told you dear
Would you really give a toss?
And then I remembered that
I have not said a word
I'd only mouthed it
To myself
Nothing's wrong, darling!
I said.

Deep Blue

The wind

The wind blows the rubbish
Around and around the court yard
Forever beating it up
The rain it came down sideways
Hitting the window like a clumsy child
With a ball
But the wind in the court yard
Is just a precursor for the big blow
It comes down the valley like a torrent
Destroying everything in its path
Pulling at roofs
And worrying crops
It was a bad wind that blows today
Today is owned by the wind
It's a bad wind that blows.

Baby Zzzz's

Crying baby of the night
Don't worry child
It will be all right
Like me, you heard the baby sing
The meaning lost, don't mean a thing
Forgotten cost
And freezing frost
I wish that I was very posh
Then I could sleep right through the night
And there wouldn't be a baby fight
,,It's your turn love
You know the score
This baby life is not a bore
Oh, ,how I wish that I could snore."

Deep Blue

Before You Die

Have you ever seen,
Really seen
A sun rise?
Set your clock
And go outside
Sit your bum down
And close your eyes
And wait,
That first sharp needle of light
The diamond light
Rules from the horizon
Then
Oh, God!
An explosion of glorious light
Heavenly sight,
Earth reborn
Then think of the endless times
The sun has risen
But each time is different
Everyone should see this sight
Just once before you die
So don't waste your life
And set you clock and go outside.

Deep Blue Cove

She whispered in my ear
I'm so far from love
Tear back my soul
Lead me not to the edge
Just tell me a liar
Because love runs deep
In me
And in me
For me
For ever
Until death breaks this spell.

Deep Blue

Dry Eyes

I've cried so much
My eyes are dry
Sometimes I try
And make them cry
There are no more tears
Inside my soul
My tears, you see
This prison stole
But when I see
The sun again
Then maybe my eyes
Will cry again.

Colin Richard Mansell

Freedom

Drugs, my friend,
Had a hold on me
Don't look at me with sympathy
Don't take my hand
Don't carry me
Don't see the pain inside of me
I've cried so much
I cannot see
Because drugs, my friend,
Are killing me
I was clean and white
When I was young
Before my junkie life began
Brown or white
I don't care
Jet black teeth
And grease hair
Soon, my friend,
I just won't care
Just wait and see
But at least, my friend, I'll be free!

Deep Blue

God's Breath

The spirit of the wind
Enlightenment of man
Creation speaks to me
I stand there for I am
A capsule full of light
The spark within the night
The dark before the dawn
A mother's rage full scorn
A gritting of the teeth
The sweat resting on my brow
The sweet smell of peace
The glory that is man.

Hard Life

The twisted life of a hardworking man
He tries his best
To do the best that he can
He gets up at seven everyday
Apart from Sundays
When his mowing the hay
His wife doesn't love him
His boys don't know
He is the man with the money
Is that all that I am?

Deep Blue

Ice Cream Earth

Shoot the moon
Melt the sun
Drown the sea
Blow the wind
Dig the Earth
Because the earth is cool
If you look at the Earth
From outer space
It looks as if it is
Topped with ice cream
How odd is that
It's cool
So dig the Earth man.

Diana

Diana, I think an angel you are
With sensitive eyes and a magical charm
Just one look from you is all that I need
To make me start shaking and go weak at the knees
Diana, to me, a real woman you are
With a kind sense of purpose
You shine like a star
If ever the day that you need me ,my love
I will come running
With a heart full of love
I wish that I knew you
For all of my life
One day sweetest Diana
You'll make a fabulous wife.

Deep Blue

Little Bird

My darling
I saw a bird outside my bars
Small and blue with silver wings
I looked at her and she did sing
I ask that she would do for me,
A noble favour if she pleased
To fly across the sky so blue
To find my love, my love so true
And land upon an apple tree
To see my love, my love for me
And sing a song of love and truth
If you my love knew how I hurt
I'm sure that you would find for me
A place beside your apple tree.

Sailing

When we sail across the sea
To find a world we've never seen
The weather might be wild and cruel
So bide your time and stay real cool
Because making new ways in the sun
And second chances can be won
Stay bright and strong and you will see
The wind will sail you across the sea
The wind of change.

Deep Blue

The Ambulance

The traffic light, it turned red
And in the back the girl was dead
The driver stopped at the red light
He turned his sirens off that night
There was no point in going fast
The same old story from the past
He radios he is coming in
With Jane Doe dead
Oh what a sin
She was only 17 you see
She should have gone home for her tea
Instead she bought two brown, one white
And overdosed that very night

The black teeth boy

The drug filled boy
Was full of crack
Dirty face and bad bad back
Hands that soap had never seen
And teeth so black they can't be cleaned
He never has a pound on him
There's always stubble on his chin
He lives each day just as it comes
At twelve o'clock he meets his chums
They go out thieving every day
It is a wicked game they play
He does not give a toss for you
That drug filled boy what will he do.

Deep Blue

The three musketeers

Last time I saw you
Was there in court
Thank you my darling for all your support
All the time that you spent thinking of me
Is giving me strength and dignity
The letters you wrote
The money you sent
Is keeping me strong
You don't know what this meant
It meant that I was made to be thrown in prison, you see
Soon I will see you
And then we will be
Together again the way it should be
Me you and thebaby
The three musketeers
So stay strong my darling
And see through those tears.

Morning Breaks

Sun does rise
I look in the mirror
And see my son in my eyes
Lunch time comes
I sit alone
Embarrassingly eating
All alone
I watch the clock
It ticks away
Can't wait until the end of day
I travel home
All on my own
Still I eat all alone
My heart it cries
For a friend indeed
One friend you see is all I need.

Deep Blue

Faith

Cold as ice,
Sour like a lemon,
Prickly as a thorn
Damn those stinging nettles.
Life can be like this
Where is all the bliss?
Where is all the joy?
Life treats me like a toy
Maybe one day, soon,
My life will take a turn
And I don't feel the burn, of life
If you haven't felt the pain
Then you'll never feel the joy
Because truth is love, you see,
And still water runs real deep
Keep your faith my friend
And you'll make it to the end
Truth is love.

My belly hurts

Just because of love
The sort of love you dream about
When you're sitting drinking tea,
When you fall in love
Deep as can be
When you touch and squeeze
You pull each other so, so tight
Your lips entwined delight
When you push for the very first time
But only half way in, I wait for you to pull me in
Deep as can be two people at that moment become one
Wet and deep
Never to part
And never apart again
I love you so much
My belly hurts.

Deep Blue

Why don't you love me anymore?

Oh... Why don't you love me anymore?
Your smile gives you away, you see,
I can't get over how much you mean to me.
I don't want to be free,
I don't want to be me,
It's me and you my dove
This spell was made from love
Why don't you love me anymore?
I can't imagine me without you
Oh... what in God name will I do?
I want to be together again
I want everything to stay the same
Oh... Why don't you love me anymore?
I will scream and cry and try to die,
I will self harm
And throw away my lucky charm
Why don't you love me anymore?
You stupid whore
Please my love
I didn't mean that line above
Just give me love
Hell why don't you snug me anymore?
Or kiss me,
Or miss me,
Or can't resist me
Why don't you love me anymore?

My first car

It was mean,
It was clean
It had a go faster stripe
And a big fat exhaust
And it went like a kite
My first car
The back seat had no springs
They got bounced out on night
By the loveliest angel
A big fat delight
She had breasts big and round
She pushes me to the ground
And had me
In my first car
I love her,
She loves me
With my car
That made three.

Deep Blue

My love

My love,
My life,
My loving wife,
Take leave of me
But only to make yourself
More beautiful
Then tend to me, quench my thrust
And then love me,
Come to me,
Give me your all.
I will watch your eyes
Glisten in delight
I will feel you quieter
And bend to my will
Sweat, sweat love.
And in the morning
You will be my wife once more
And you will be
A pure white mother again.

Come dance with me

Come dance with me
Young playful girl
Come dance the dance of love.
Tread carefully and you will see
You turn from child to woman
Oh... take my hand
And we will dance,
We'll dance until the dawn
I will show to you true love my dear
A love that's made in heaven.
We will gaze at each other's eyes
I will see no more
But you
And when the dance ends
We will stay embraced
For ever spell bound
Together In heaven once more.

Deep Blue

I love you no matter what

Listen to me play for you
The beat is the beat of your heart,
Some may come and stay awhile
But I will be here forever
I will cushion you from all life's troubles
And shelter you from the rain
I would fight and die for you
In heart as it is in heaven.
There is nothing I would not do for you
No sea I would not cross
I would find you if the clocks stood still
I would bear upon my cross
For one kiss, just one, my love
I would give every penny
That I've ever earn
So be with me
Until the end
Our love just can't be wrong.

Poor women of vanity cross

A husband sits
And old wife nits
And the cat sits licking his bits
And everything is well
In the house at vanity cross
They was young once long ago
They made love once long ago
A match made in heaven
So long ago
She could not bear a child
So the man brought the woman a cat
It was out of love you know
Now she loves that cat
Just like a child
It is a sight to be seen
The cat is the queen
So, so long ago.

Deep Blue

Be you

I sit with screwed up face,
Face out of joint
Eyes full of rage
Fed up with life,
Fed up with me
And fed up with you.
Chase away the blues
Dry the tears of life
So what if you don't conform
So what if you have weeds on your lawn
Just be happy, just be you.

The Lord in the field

In a field by the big oak tree
Is a grave marked with two sticks
In the shape of Gods cross
A simple grave this grave it is
Nor garnished with flowers
Or granite or stone
The man inside
He sleeps alone

The sun seams to shine on him
The sun seams to shine from him
On this patch of the field
Funny because it was not known for its weather
And clever men say
That a Lord does lay there
In the sun kissed Conner
Of Gods own field.

Perhaps he was a bad, bad Lord
Who causes all kinds of pane,
So they buried him here
All out on his own
In a cold Conner of the field
Where no one would tend to the dark Lords grave
Where good people will forget.

But I like to think him a good kind man
So they buried him here in this field,
So they buried him here
Where the suns at its best
It shines and warms him
Right down to his chest.

Deep Blue

And the light keeps the bad sprits away
I will let my children play in the field
The field of the Lord
The Lord's field.

Oh Mighty Wind

Oh mighty wind
Sometimes you blow death
But sometimes you are the wind of change
The wind in our sails
That brings me down
To my knees
I look at you
But you can't be seen
At all
Oh mighty wind
I think I'm most scared
Of the wind of change
The changing winds
Of time
If only the clock could be turned back
I could save our souls
For sure
Father time
Is good to me
Time to change.

Deep Blue

Gloom

A wild untouched forest
Mighty trees
You stole the sky
Why do you live in this gloom?
Like me I too live in the gloom
The twilight
But unlike you
I one day hope to be free
A woman stole my sky
I was lost in the woods
But now I've seen a chink of light
And I am now on the way to my freedom
But I have lost a piece of my heart
There was a time when I might stay
In the forest
The light became too bright
But now my eyes can see again.

Tattered life

Tattered life,
Sunny days
In the park
I hope and pray
Just waking up
Among the clouds
I see the shapes
How tall my tower
The darker, the clouds
The more it rains
As long as the day
Is not the same
When you have had
A would of stuff
You realise
You don't need that much
One cup, one plate
One knife, one fork
Is all you need?
For your support.

Deep Blue

Alive again

Look how nature laughs
As I walk by,
Look how the sky darkens
I can hear myself think
I plant seeds in my head
They grow more vigorously
Then ever before now
Thank God for change
And change thanks God
Drink deeply now
It's safe to be alive again.

Colin Richard Mansell

Poem from the heart of a dad

Don't think of me bad my sons
Every man drops a note sometimes
Just be strong
Just get along with life
Life's a funny fish you know
Sometimes you just can't let it go
Somehow you think you're in control
It splits your very mind and soul
If you did wrong just once my son
Then people think you bad for life
Did you help the granny cross?
I think I even liked my boss
And as for ever getting on with life
I left my school a man I am
I worked so hard, I broke my knees
On life.
My loving wife got rid of me
My kids you know I never see
This life it nearly broke my back
I thought I'd had a heart attack
Life had a king
I had a jack
That life
Maybe, someday, soon
I'll brake out from my dark cocoon
The sky will turn back bright and blue
I look forward my sons to being with you.

I hurt so bad all the time
My heart burns
It's never my turn
Shame on me
Please excuse me
I'm so sorry
It never gets better

Deep Blue

Justice is an illusion
That stinks
To high heaven
It's the wrong colour
To short not big enough
The last in line
Never on time
No peace of mind
Failed m.o.t
I got a hair in my tea
You don't believe me
I'm full of negativity
The funny thing is
It never used to be like this
I used to love hair in my tea
And you being with me
Love in the park
Hopping the gate after dark
Be quiet don't make the dog bark
I hope she comes on
It hasn't been long
How we used to get along
Singing the same song of life

What do you see?

Look into the fire
Open fire
With open eyes
Look deep
Intense
Warm your hands
And warm your soul
Watch the flames dance
Each flame climbing on the back
Of the one below
Josser ling for position
Then watch as the fire
Burns low and crackles
Glowing like the sun
Look into the fire
What do you see?

Deep Blue

Fathers for justice

Run along the egged with me
I'll go first I am brave
Just watch the way I balance and run
Your not as good as me, me ,me
I look down, I don't care
I have nothing to lose, you see,
My boys have gone
My eyes still red
My wife as cut me off you see
I can't get close
She saw to that
She told some lies
Mud sticks to me
She used the courts
She used the police
I got treated like a thief
All it takes is one phone call
And a bunch of lies
With stories so tall
She can say most anything
Just like a bird
She sings
I think attention she does seek
That's why she built me like a thief.
She said that I did beat on her
But twenty years without matter
No police had ever felt my cloth
In my road my house was so posh
A carpet shop
And a house half paid
My wages weekly I did save
My two babies were nursed
Fat and fat spoiled
They had everything
Money could buy

But it wasn't enough
For her to give me some love
Not one single touch
Or a kiss on the brow
I sleep in a bed that our marriage did vole
All on my own night after night
Its no wonder this mess
Lead to a fight
She phoned the police
And then using the courts
She got me band
From my very roots
Each time I could not stand it
The pain got too much
Did march to my house
With my dad flag of Corse
But she never ever
Opened the door
Instead phoned up piglet once more
And it was back into the cell
I couldn't take it
It was hell
That's when my mind broke
Because of the pain
I just couldn't take
Anymore strain
The pain, the pain it toys with me
Its two years now without my sons
I sit and look at what I've done.
Small wind

I lay in the park
I have to squint to see
Lovely small wind
Is blowing on me
I love the summer
More than life itself

Deep Blue

It's good for your mind
And good for your health
All I want is six
Or maybe eight good weeks
How I love the summer
Small wind blowing on me.

I've seen the earth

I've seen the earth
From deep out in space
When I looked out the port hole
God took over my face
It was blue
It was green
It was great
It's the earth
It was mine
One way the sun set
One way the sun rise
Oh... I've seen the earth
From deep out in space
Just at that moment
God appeared on my face.

Deep Blue

More than

More than life
More than love
More than angels
And heaven
From high up above
More than fear
So be brave
Else your take your fear
Straight to the grave
Don't be late
Let sleeping dogs lie
Wave really hard
It may be your last good bye
Take a chance
Live your life
Take pride in your kids
But don't trust your wife
Just be kind
To yourself
But most of all
Don't sit on the shelf.

Colin Richard Mansell

High like a bird

Love me
Want me
Fly high like the bird
Your grip is strong
But don't break me
Why is it when I'm on my own?

I see lights in my mind
And you sit on your throne
You look down on me
Like mud on your shoe
If I was free
The things I would do.

Take strength in my verse
Young untouched man
Just try to do things
The best that you can
Never pass beauty
Without taking a look
When you go to a library
Try reading a book

Look up at the stars
Look deep in the night
Dream dreams of love
And of fine paradise
Live long and prosper
Taste every bit
A make sure you cuddle
Your girl though the night
Advice is so easy
For me to give you

Deep Blue

It's easy to tell
A young man what to do
You're young and you're nerveless
But it's not a mistake

Put your cakes in the oven
But don't over bake
Turn down the heat
Before it's too late.

Anger

Boiling up
Inside of me
Angers got a hold on me
I clench my fists
I grit my teeth
It bubbles up from beneath
Blood red eyes
Groans and sighs
Don't come to close
Don't tell me lies
Boiling up
Inside of me
Angers got a hold on me.

Deep Blue

Love me love me not

Do you love me?
Bet you don't
I love you
I always have
You to me are love itself
You'd never get left
Upon life's shelf.

Your pretty hair
And piercing stair
You make me feel
Like I don't care
So do you love me?
The way I love you
I love you like a man consumed.

Consumed with love
But always in fear
If you take your love from here
Be true to me
My darling girl
I taste you
And I love your smell.

Your open arms
Your candid charms
My soul will dance
Within your arms
I love you
Do you love me?
Because I think
We was meant to be
But if by chance
Your love does fade
I might start to misbehave

Colin Richard Mansell

I'll kick and scream
And pull your hair
Without your love
I just won't care

My heart will die
I'll start to cry
With heavy soul
You hear me sigh
So do you love me?
I hope you do
Just the way that I love you.

Deep Blue

You breathe I breath

I am the very air you breathe
I am your first kiss
I am your dawn
I am the breath on your neck
I am the sparkle in your eyes
I will become your paradise.

I am the sun on your back
I am our baby's first smack
The smack that brings in life
You are my dream wife
I am a thousand solders cries
I am the earth that lies.

That lies at the feet of man
I am the kiss of life
You may call my name at night
I am the one that welcomed you
One and one is two.

Colin Richard Mansell

Life is a sunrise

Life is a sunrise
But you need to get up
Don't stay in bed
Or you miss the sun up
Be smart and true
You know what to do.

But you need to get up
Else you'll miss to much
I wish life was a sunrise
There wouldn't be any pain
At the moment you see
Every day is the same
I just can't get up.

Day turns into night
To get out of bed
Is a terrible fight
I think it's depression
That ales me this way.

I feel very sad
But I just have to say
That life is a sunrise
So you need to get up
But don't stay in bed
Or you'll miss the sun up.

Can you see me?
I am here
Look in the corner
Don't look over there
So can you see me?
I'm good looking
And dashing

Deep Blue

And if you're good looking too
I'll start spending my cash
Still can't see me
Perhaps I'm not really here
I stay on my own
And I'll sink in my beer.

www.ingramcontent.com/pod-product-compliance
Ingram Content Group UK Ltd.
Pitfield, Milton Keynes, MK11 3LW, UK
UKHW041412180426
11947UKWH00007B/77